COMMUNICATION & CORPORATE ETIQUETTE

(INCLUDING GROOMING FOR TODAY'S BUSINESS WORLD)

GITANGSHU ADHIKARY

Made with ♥ on the Notion Press Platform
www.notionpress.com

To my wife (Krishna) and my son (Chandramouli).

They inspired me to write this book.

Contents

Foreword

The origin of this book is actually my source of inspiration that came about while talking to my son, Chandramouli. He has always maintained that grooming, communication, and etiquette are three basic necessities required to succeed in the professional and business world.

Krishna, my wife, has mentioned time and again that empathetic communication, coupled with compassion and understanding, can actually create a beautiful and congenial atmosphere wherever a person is, and in whatever that person does.

Their thoughts have remained in my mind, and over the years I have seen a lot of astonishing situations that have made my yearning to write on communication, grooming, and etiquette so much more compelling.

The needs of today's business world, and the people in it, have also been other reasons to have driven me to have written this book.

Preface

Communication acts as the main support for any organization to function smoothly. Every employee within the organization needs to know What to do and not do when it comes to corporate communication.

Along with communication, grooming and appearance do make a difference in the environment that the employee is in.

These two, coupled with corporate etiquette, help to maintain good relationships on the one hand, while also helping to maximize performance and productivity of all employees.

Acknowledgements

Although writing a book can be much harder and intimidating than we usually imagine, it is definitely a truly rewarding experience overall. Writing this book would have been impossible without my wife, Krishna, and my son, Chandramouli, who have always stood by me for as long as I can remember. They have always been the best examples of what a really good family is all about, and I can never thank them enough no matter however much I try. My deepest love and prayers for both of them. I thank God to have blessed me with so many supportive people around me - but most of all, Krishna and Chandramouli.

CHAPTER ONE

Communication

Defining Communication

The exchange of information, knowledge, and ideas that takes place between the sender and receiver through an accepted set of codes symbols, and language is what communication is all about.

Understanding Communication

the use of code, language, and symbols to transmit an exchange ideas, knowledge, and information which creates a basic mutual understanding, is known as communication.

Even after the exchange or transmission of these symbols and codes, if there is still no mutual understanding, no communication is said to have taken place at all.

The entire process of communication must include the following elements to make it truly effective:

- there must be a source that initiates communication through various codes, symbols, and expressions
- the entire set of codes, symbols, and expressions must be encoded in a definite way that is easy for the recipient to understand
- a definite message needs to be expressed to the recipient so that the actual idea or information is relayed
- a medium must exist for true communication to take place
- decoding of the entire set of codes symbols and expressions at the recipient's end must be possible so as to make it easy for the recipient to understand
- there must be a destination that receives the communication via various codes, symbols, and expressions
- it is imperative that noise is reduced to the minimum so that no confusion of any sort is created, and the recipient in understands the communique clearly
- the feedback from the recipient end to the initiator end is known as feedback, which is also called reply

CHAPTER TWO

Types of Communication

We've already discussed that communication is the process of exchanging and sharing information, ideas, and messages between various parties within a particular time and place.

Primarily, there are two types of communication:

- Verbal Communication
- Non-verbal Communication

Verbal Communication

Verbal communication involves the exchange of ideas, information, messages, and thoughts by using verbal or spoken words. Again,verbal communication can be of two types:

- Oral Communication
- Written Communication

Non-verbal Communication

Non-verbal communication involves the exchange of ideas, information, messages, and thoughts by using any means other than speech, like hand gestures, facial epressions, and so on. Types of non-verbal signals:

- Chronemics - also known as Time Signals
- Haptics - better known as Touch Signals
- Kinesics - also called Body Sygnals
- Proxemics - these are Space Signals
- Artifacts - these are Body Signals
- Personal Appearance

The Barriers That Affect Effective Communication From Taking Place

Some of the reasons why effective communication doesn't take place most of the time are:

The different backgrounds that the receiver and the sender come from can hinder effective communication between them.

More often, the messages conveyed without words (nonverbal communication) can actually project wrong signals, thereby creating more miscommunication rather than effective communication.

The situation where communication takes place can also affect its effectiveness in adverse ways that cannot be explained immediately.

Sometimes the quality of the content in the message can actually portray something totally different from what the sender of the message actually wants to say, thereby creating more confusion than effective communication.

Quite often we find that the speakers speaking skills hinder effective communication from taking place.

The listening skills of the receiver are also quite crucial. Without good aural skills, a message can be misinterpreted to create absolute miscommunication.

Some other factors that may create a barrier to effective communication taking place are Noise, Distraction, Sound, etc.

Methods To Overcome The Barriers To Communication

Here are some of the ways to overcome the barriers to communication.

The differences in perception of both the sender and the receiver of the message should be eliminated completely. Not only will this remove any barrier to communication but will also ensure that communication becomes effective.

The sender of the message must use simple language so that the receiver of the message understands it in its entirety. This helps in ensuring that there is a clear understanding between the two sides.

Noise levels of any sort must be eliminated completely so that effective communication actually takes place.

The receiver of the message should be able to listen actively so as to understand the complete message. Without a clear understanding of what the sender of the message is trying to say there cannot be any kind of effective communication at all.

The emotional state of both the sender and the receiver of the messages should be in a state where both parties are able to focus more on the topic itself. this helps communication to take place effectively.

The organizational structure should be kept as simple as possible for communication to be truly effective.

For communication to be effective it is imperative that both parties avoid any sort of information overload, lest there be confusion rather than communication.

it is judicious to give constructive feedback on any topic or point rather than simply discuss it in vague terms and leave it as it is.

Selecting the proper media for your communication is a crucial factor to ensure that communication is effective. The medium of communication must be accepted by both parties.

It pays off to ensure that flexibility in meeting the targets is implemented prudently. Give a lot of time and give both parties ample scope to be able to formulate their next line of messages to the other party.

Significance Of Communication In Everyday Life

Communication is not only important in our everyday life, but it also has a strong significance in our day-to-day life and activities. Here are some of the factors that make communication so significant in our daily life:

Communication is required for the transfer of ideas and expressions between two parties in a conducive environment.

To interact with society, it is imperative that proper communication takes place effectively.

Communication is the most crucial factor in the field of education and also extensively educates the receiver of the concepts, messages, and ideas.

Communication is really important if one wishes to keep themselves updated on a particular topic or field.

Even in the field of entertainment, communication is a really important factor.

Communication is also required for entertaining oneself.

To understand the world as a whole, it is imperative that one exhaustively communicates with, and about, their surroundings to get back replies to their queries.

Importance Of Communication In Various Activities

Communication becomes significant in various activities. Here are some activities where communication it's really significant:

Effective communication is imperative when discussing lessons in a classroom. This is true for both the instructor and the students.

Business communication has to be effective, and without effective business communication, no business can flourish at all.

Communication is really significant when it comes to acting. One must be able to effectively communicate with the concept or character through acting skills, voice modulations, expressions, etc.

Singing is another activity where communication must be effective otherwise the entire idea of the composition will not be well received.

Even in poetry, communication is quite significant, especially since the poet's ideas and concepts about a particular topic need to be communicated to the reader in such a way that the recipient does not have any kind of confusion about the topic.

When talking with peers it is crucial that one communicates glibly.

Communication is significant in other fields as well, such as judging, training, teaching, etc.

5 Types of Communication

Let us now understand the 5 types of communication briefly.

- ***Extrapersonal Communication***

Extrapersonal communication is set to take place between humans and other nonhuman entities. In this type of communication, it is crucial that there is a clear understanding between the sender and the receiver of the message. More often, the receiver of the message responds through sign language when the sender communicates a particular message.

- ***Intrapersonal Communication***

When communication takes place within an individual it is known as interpersonal communication. Usually, the sender is a part of your system - your mind or your body. The receiver is usually the brain, and it is the brain that responds to the messages that it receives.

- ***Interpersonal Communication***

interpersonal communication takes place among a set of people. When the interaction takes place between two parties who are formally or informally connected to each other, the communication will also be other family or informal. Interpersonal communication is dependent upon a number of factors such as the relationship between the two parties, the psychology of each party, the psychometric set up between the two parties, etc.

- ***Organizational Communication***

Organizational communication it's set to take place through two types of channels: formal channels and informal channels.

*Formal channels:*The three formal channels of communication are downward, upward, and horizontal.

The downward channel flows from higher to lower levels. The subordinates usually react most effectively to matters that usually seem of great interest to their boss. In this type of communication selective screening is a problem. Some examples of the downward channels are memos, procedures, policies, etc.

The upward channel on the other hand flows from the lower levels to the higher levels. In this type of communication, the employees usually need the opportunities to be heard and yet remain anonymous. this is the most ineffective of the three channels of formal communication. Some examples of the upward channels are corporate intranets, Internet, in house communication channels.

The horizontal channel communication flows among staff at the same level. This type of communication usually involves people of the same rank sending and receiving messages relevant to them and their departments.

Informal channels: The communication that takes place between various parties within an organization does not necessarily have to follow the formal pathways at all times. Today, a multitude of organizations have implemented extensive networks so that informal communications can take place effectively.

The managerial level should use these informal channels to benefit the various plans, policies, and programs, especially since informal channels are ingrained into the entire organizational life in today's business.

The three informal channels of communication are:

internal operational channel - where all communication that takes place within an organization falls under this category;

external operational channel - where all work-related communication takes place with people who are external to the organization; and,

personal channel - where all communication within the organization takes place without any particular purpose or relevance to the organization.

- ***<u>Mass Communication</u>***

Mass communication takes place via mass media such as journals, television, newspapers, books, etc. It is imperative that the sender uses a medium or mediator to transmit the various messages, ideas, and information that they wish to transmit to the mass of receivers who they target.

CHAPTER THREE

About Assertive Communication

Assertive communication means expressing one's point of view in a way that is both direct and clear while respecting others as well. Assertive communication helps to minimize conflict and also to control any anger or inhibition. It is a means to create a more conducive, frank, and free atmosphere among the parties involved in the communication.

The Fundamental Principles Of Assertive Communication

Some of the key principles of assertive communication are:

- Practice: Practice is necessary for assertive communication.
- Flexibility: Tailor your communication approach to the circumstance and recipient.

- Skill: The ability to communicate effectively is a skill, not a psychological trait.
- Retreat, recharge, return: Take a break from the talk and retreat, recharge, and then return. Unwind, reconsider, and then try again.
- Connection: Connection is a key focus of assertive communication, which develops the other MRT characteristics.

Final Verdict Up Front

Let's get to the bottom line right away:

- To help build connections, assertive communication is essential.
- Building connections through assertive communication can help you handle issues by remaining controlled, clear, and confident.

Applications Of Assertive Communication

- When is it appropriate or inappropriate to use assertive communication in a particular environment?
- Why is assertive communication difficult?
- How will using assertive communication improve your relationships?

Skill Set In Communication

The three primary aspects of any communication skill set are:

- Assertive Communication: Express yourself politely and clearly.
- Active constructive response: React to people in order to establish long-lasting bonds.
- Adulation: Accolades help increase proficiency and winning streaks.

Aggressive Communication

The following are constituents that make for aggressive communication:

- Must have the last word
- Talking over the other person
- Out-of-control emotion
- Blaming
- Talking down

Reasons For Aggressive Communication

Some of the underlying justifications that give rise to aggressive communication:

- An effective offense is the best defense.
- If you want to succeed, you must be assertive and vocal.
- Never give up in a fight.
- Any indication of vulnerability will lead to your exploitation.
- I deserve it and desire it right away, right now.

Passive Communication

The main constituents of passive communication are:

- Quiet: The subject remains quiet mostly.
- No eye contact: Subjects avert any eye contact at all.
- Withdrawn: The subject seems withdrawn during the major part of the conversation.
- Sulking: In many cases, the subjects seem to be sulking.
- Submissive: Passive communicators are usually more submissive.
- Fearful: Most passive communicators have been found to be fearful.
- Appeasing: This type of person tends to pacify or placate someone by acceding to their demands.

Reasons For Passive Communication

Some of the underlying reasons that constitute passive communication:

- It always seems wrong to complain or refute.
- The subject usually doesn't care. it simply doesn't make any difference.
- Most of the time the person feels that they will make enemies if they speak their mind.
- This type of person has a misconception that nothing and no one ever changes in any case.
- Rather than being correct, they give more importance to others liking them.
- they always avoid conflict, especially since that is what makes them passive in the first place.

The 3 Cs Of assertive communication

The 3 Cs of assertive communication are:

- Confidence: The person is usually composed and confident that they have the ability to handle the situation.
- Clarity: The message must not be exaggerated in any way. It must be delivered as simply as possible and must be easy to understand.
- Control: Always keep track of the other people and constantly take hints from their body language and

attitude. Whenever required, modulate the delivery of your communication.

Reasons That Hinder The 3 Cs

Some of the reasons and misconceptions that hinder the 3 Cs are:

- Most of the time the subject thinks that they are not strong.
- The subject feels that they don't measure up.
- Their weaknesses always seem to outweigh their strengths.

Reasons That Promote The 3 Cs

Some of the reasons that truly promote the 3Cs are:

- The belief that it can be worked out.
- Mutual trust and respect promote the 3 Cs readily.
- The assurance that one can express oneself clearly and confidently.
- What the subject believes truly matters.

The IDEAL Model

First, let us understand the constituents of the IDEAL model:

- I - Identify: To identify and understand the problem.
- D - Describe: To describe the problem accurately and objectively.
- E - Express: To express one's concerns and feelings whenever appropriate.
- A - Ask: Ask for the other's perspective and take on the topic/problem, and also ask for a reasonable change/modification as well.
- L - List: List the outcomes of all the above in a lucid and structured manner.

Tips on IDEAL

- I: Identify & determine the issue, comprehend it, and look out for thinking traps. Find icebergs (if necessary). Put It In Context (if necessary). Only after this step has been taken care of does actual communication take place.
- D: Describe the issue factually, accurately, and objectively. Be specific, use recent events. Give/Use facts on who, what, when, and where. Avoid any exaggeration.
- E: Express descriptively your worries, concerns, and feelings (if appropriate). Use "I" instead of "You" as

much as possible. Minimize exaggeration.

- A: Ask for the viewpoint of the other person. Instead of asking "Why", ask "What" and "How". To be sure you heard them correctly, repeat back what you heard, and take confirmation on it. Finally, request a "Good Faith" adjustment that is appropriate (reasonable, doable, and workable). Aim for a win-win situation.
- L: List the results. Emphasize more on the positive as opposed to the negative. Think about appropriateness as well.

How To Practice Assertive Communication

Here is what you can do - using 4 different scenarios - to practice assertive communication:

- Practice assertive communication with your group in both Scenarios 1 and 2. While individual 1 starts assertive communication, individual 2 answers/ responds by staying within the role-play.
- Practice assertive communication with a partner in Scenario 3.
- Practice using the IDEAL concept in your own situation in Scenario 4.

Check Your Learning So Far

- About the skill: Communication that is Clear, Confident, and Controlled can be called Assertive Communication.
- Time to use it: Asserive Communication should be used mostly when the need to confront someone arises - especially with regard to a conflict, challenge, or issue. It has been proven to be the best mode of communication during such situations, especially since it helps to address the issue and also resolve the situation effectively, almost immediately.
- How to use it: Resort to using the IDEAL model. I - Identify and understand the problem; D - Describe the problem accurately and objectively; E - Express your feelings and concerns frankly (when appropriate); A - Ask the other person to express their perspective, and then request them for a reasonable change; and, L - List the outcomes and results.

Reality Is Equal To Perception

There are two stages of perception:

- Initial perception - where the perception is almost immediate.
- Sustained perception - where the perception is created over time.

Initial And Sustained Perception

The constituents of Initial Perception are:

Presence

- Appearance
- Manner & Style
- Etiquette
- Awareness

Presentation

- Listening & Interpersonal Skills
- Meeting Skills
- Business Meals and Occasions

The constituents of Sustained Perception are:

Professionalism & Personal Substance

- Attitude
- Civility
- Work Ethics
- Discipline
- Integrity

CHAPTER FOUR

Appearance & Grooming

Appearance & grooming are essential if you wish to create a truly positive impact in your professional environment. While dressing can create on your self, it can also do the same to your colleagues and even your clientele.

What you wear conveys whether or not you are Presentable, Sincere, Ambitious, Confident, etc. After all, you won't get another chance to recreate the first impression.

Grooming Standards For Men

Some grooming standards that men should know and follow:

Hair

- The hair on your neck and the collar of your shirt mustn't meet.
- If you use hair color, make sure that it looks natural, and also compliments you.

- Always keep the hair trimmed around the neck and above the ears.

Face

- Make sure you shave daily.
- If you have a mustache or beard, make sure you trim it regularly.
- Never let the mustache grow beyond the corners of your mouth.

Sideburns

- Keep your sideburns well-trimmed.
- The length of your sideburns must not go below the mid-point of your ears.
- The sideburns should not be too wide.

Belt

- Don't wear belts that are too long that they act like wraparounds on your waist.
- Make sure that the belt you wear suits your dress code.
- Wearing a belt that matches your shoes, or your wristwatch.

Shoes

- Keep your shoes polished at all times.
- Black formal shoes with laces are a great choice.
- Never wear high heels. standard and low heels go appropriately with your formal attire.

Tie

- The tie is an integral part of your formal attire and must be formal, not flashy.
- Make sure that you put a dimple at the base of your knot.
- Don't wear a tie that's too wide or too narrow. an average-width tie is the safest bet anytime, anywhere.

Socks

- Never wear flashy socks.
- Turkish or thick materials don't really blend well with formal wear.
- Wear solid colors only.

Handkerchief

- Carry a handkerchief in your trouser pocket.
- Though a solid color handkerchief is the best choice, you may use one that is slightly dotted or striped - at the edges mainly.
- Don't use Turkish, woolen, or thick handkerchiefs. a simple minimalist cotton or silk handkerchief can create wonders.

Watch

- The watch must be of good quality.
- Remember that flashy or sporty watches fail to create any impactful impression in a formal/official atmosphere.
- What may ultimately do the trick is a simple watch with straight, classy lines.

Dos For Men

Here are some of the things that men must do:

- Maintain a professional look at all times.
- Attire yourself to create a lasting impression on your audience.
- Wear outfits that fit you well.
- Ensure that your clothing is ironed.
- Basic collars and cuffs on shirts are crucial.
- A formal yet basic wristwatch can create wonders.
- Your hair must be well-cut and nicely trimmed.
- The use of delicate scents, perfumes, and deodorants will be appreciated.
- Wear conservative ties, which should come to the middle of your belt buckle.
- Black lace-up shoes go well with a suit. They make formal attire more complete.
- Hair should not reach the top of your shirt collar. Make sure to part your hair neatly.

Don'ts For Men

Here are some of the things men mustn't do:

- Keep your shirt's buttons to a minimum.
- Useless clothing should not be worn.

- Do not dress in wrinkled garments.
- Avoid having hair that covers your eyebrows or falls in your face.
- Do not wear shirts with short sleeves.
- Wear long or calf-height socks.
- Avoid perfume that has a strong, distant scent.
- Skip the garish ties.
- Avoid wearing large, shiny belt buckles, clips, or tie pins.
- When wearing a tie, avoid unbuttoning the top shirt button.
- Avoid donning loafers with a suit.

Grooming Standards For Women

Some grooming standards that women should know and follow:

Hair

- Clean, well-shaped, and put together in a polished, feminine manner.
- Avoid using obvious combs, rubber bands, and pins.
- Never let your hair show anything informal.

Makeup

- Applying makeup properly will allow the colors to complement natural skin tones and highlight facial characteristics.
- Lipstick colors should be tasteful and flatter the wearer.
- Never wear long artificial eyelashes on a regular basis.

Jewellery

- Especially when wearing a uniform, wear just one ring. A wedding ring is acceptable.
- Necklaces shouldn't protrude past the shirt collar.
- Male employees are not permitted to wear earrings. Minimalist designs might be acceptable for women though.
- Body piercing is not considered appropriate, especially when wearing a uniform. For ladies, perhaps only earrings are permitted.

Dos For Women

Here are some of the things that women must do:

- Look professional at all times.
- Adapt your attire to the audience.
- Wear outfits that fit you well.
- Make sure your clothing is neatly ironed.
- Maintain your hair, and keep it well-cut and nicely trimmed.
- Dress formally and accessorize with heels (up to 1 1/2" to 2") that have a high vamp.
- That is what will make it appropriate with your formal attire.
- Discreet business attire.
- Focus on your lips and eyes.
- Apply lip color correctly.
- A basic manicure is the best manicure.

Don’ts For Women

Here are some of the things women mustn’t do:

- Avoid donning dark clothing.
- Avoid wearing wrinkled garments.
- Keep transparent clothing away from your wardrobe of formalwear.
- Avoid having hair that covers your eyebrows or falls in your face.
- Avoid wearing huge, hanging earrings.
- Don’t use perfumes or deodorants that give off a strong, distant scent.
- Wearing anything excessively bright, tight, sheer, or short is not advised.
- Avoid donning open-toed footwear.
- Avoid overdoing the cosmetics.
- Don’t wear big jewellery or large, flashy buckles.

CHAPTER FIVE

Corporate Etiquette

What Is Etiquette?

A rule of conduct, known as etiquette, defines expected social behavior in accordance with current customary norms within a culture, social class, or organization.

Why business Etiquette?

- We need business etiquette to display professionalism, cultivate a polished image, and foster a sense of reliability.
- It appears like breaking every regulation is the accepted practice today!
- Unfortunately, some people aren't even aware of the guidelines regarding how we should respect one another. This may result in difficulties, annoyances, misunderstandings, and a lack of fluidity in interpersonal communications.

Some Important Business Etiquettes

Let us list a few important aspects of business etiquette:

- E-mail etiquette
- Dining etiquette
- Telephone etiquette
- Office etiquette
- Meeting etiquette
- Business card etiquette

Now, let us discuss each briefly.

E-mail Etiquette

Because email etiquette is so new, as we use it more frequently and new technologies emerge, the norms are constantly changing.

Yet, certain basic decorum should be followed because this correspondence is owned by the company.

Need For Email Etiquette

Email etiquette is needed for the following reasons primarily:

- It brings about a touch of professionalism in the email communique between the involved parties.

- Efficiency is further enhanced and ensured when email etiquette is maintained.
- Protection from any liability can be assured, especially since it is a formal scenario that the parties are involved.

------xxx------

Rules To Follow To Maintain Email Etiquette

Here are some essential rules to follow when it comes to email etiquette:

- Be direct and succinct.
- Employ appropriate grammar, spelling, and punctuation.
- Make it your own.
- Avoid the use of BCC and CCC if possible.
- Employ templates for responses that you use regularly.
- Respond right away.
- Choose a subject that has meaning and is relevant to the situation.
- Before sending the email, read it.
- Limit the number of attachments and make sure to mention them in the content.
- Be cautious while using emoticons and acronyms.
- Use HTML and rich text communications with caution.
- Employ the active voice rather than the passive one.

Dining Etiquette

Dining Etiquette

- Some points to remember regarding dining etiquette:
- Be punctual.
- Enter from your left, and stand to the right of your chair.
- In your lap, place your napkin.
- Make a quick decision on your menu options.
- Never place an order for the priciest item.
- Wait until everyone has been served before starting to eat.
- Use the appropriate silverware for the appropriate food.

------xxx------

Manners To Follow To Maintain Dining Etiquette

Here are some essential rules to follow when it comes to dining etiquette:

- Eat without stuffing your mouth.
- Unless you are eating in the European style, keep one hand in your lap.
- Use the same implement that you use to insert in your mouth when you need to remove any unwanted thing that is there (except bones).
- Eat at a steady pace.
- Strive to keep up a decent dinner conversation.
- Never take medication while dining.
- Your napkin should be placed in your chair if you have to leave the table.

Telephone Etiquette

Telephone Etiquette

Some rules to follow to maintain telephone etiquette:

- When you call, identify yourself.
- Be cordial and call the caller by his name.
- Shorten your talk.
- Never rush anything.
- Pay close attention.
- Stay quiet and listen attentively.
- Avoid eating or chewing while on the phone.
- Get his permission if you want to put the caller on wait.
- A suitable salutation should be used to end the conversation.
- Let the caller go first and hang up.
- Calls that are missed should be returned as soon as possible.
- When someone contacts you by mistake, gently let them know they have the wrong number.

------XXX------

<u>How To Manage Angry Callers</u>

- Pay close attention to their issue or concern.
- Let him complete what he is saying without interfering.
- Never remark, "You're wrong."
- Have sympathy for, and empathize with them.
- You ought to be competent in your field, look into his complaint or issue, and find a solution.
- Inform them how you resolved the issue.
- Do not deceive.
- After you have the answer, call them back; it's crucial to get their opinion.

Office Etiquette

Some Things To Remember Regarding Office Etiquette

Please remember these points when it comes to office etiquette:

People who behave properly at work are promoted and given desirable tasks.

Those who are thought to be obnoxious are passed over or have their work terminated.

Use common sense and be self-aware.

Keep your mouth shut.

Never cross your boss's authority.

Respect the dress code established by your employer.

Show the same respect to all employees.

Do not submit any offensive content.

------XXX------

Why Employees Are Fired Usually

Some common reasons why employees are fired are:

Obscene language.

Excessive office chitchat and gossip.

Drinking while at work.

Leaving or taking a break without informing anyone.

An excessive number of personal calls.

------XXX------

What Breaches Office Etiquette

Here are some activities/actions that breach office etiquette completely:

- Poor hygiene.
- Bad practices and appalling habits.
- Wastefulness - like wasteful use of paper

Meeting Etiquette

Some things to follow to maintain meeting etiquette:

- Avoid using obscene language and swearing.
- Use innuendos sparingly.
- Ineffective communication is not professional.
- In your initial meeting, refrain from becoming personal.
- The first person to the door should open it and hold it open for those who are coming behind them.
- Turn down the ringtone on your phone and just accept text and voicemail messages.

Business Card Etiquette

Some things to follow to maintain business card etiquette:

- Never go without a business card.
- Maintain it and keep it current.
- Make it available right now.
- Be judicious when distributing.
- Deliver it at the proper moment and in the right way.

Business Etiquette Postures

The Handshake

Never hold someone else's below your own. This demonstrates that you are effectively assuming control.

Never hold someone else's hand above your own. This demonstrates how easily you cede control.

When two people shake hands in a professional and appropriate fashion, it conveys that they are on equal footing and are close friends.

Avoid shaking hands too vigorously or not without any vigor at all.

------xxx------

Seating Positions

- Never seat in a position where you are bent forward.
- Even sitting erect at is not correct.
- Sit comfortably and rest your back on the backrest of the chair.
- Sitting with your arms and feet wide open shows that you are too casual.
- When you sit with one of your legs crossed over the other and keep one hand on the head of the seat, it means you are judgemental of the other person.
- Turning the chair around and sitting with the front of your body against the backrest can actually mean that you are being argumentative.

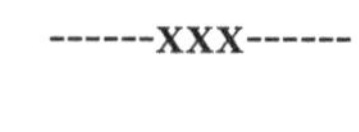

Dress Code

- Please don't wear anything that's not formal.
- Never wear shorts. trousers are a safer bet always.
- Don't wear glares or goggles.
- Avoid being dressed informally or semi-formally.
- Only dress formally.
- You may wear shades, but not too stylish.
- Dressing in solids and using two-tone for the contract/ match of colors is the best way forward.

Business Meals

Types Of Business Meals

- Breakfast Meetings: Morning meetings are frequently the most efficient time to meet with busy executives.
- Luncheon Meals: Iced tea and basic fare are served for lunch.
- After-Work Cocktail: Only one after-work cocktail is necessary to maintain control at the meeting and while driving.
- Business Dinners: the ones where **B**=Bread and **D**=Drink

------xxx------

Rules For The Host

- Avoid forcing or insisting on invitations.
- Ask for responses and confirmations as soon as you can.
- Invite others for professional purposes only, not anything personal or informal.
- Decide on a suitable environment and setting.

- Be there early to welcome your guests and invitees.
- Give the server your credit card ahead of time.
- Request that an additional 18% be added to your bill as a tip
- At the conclusion of the meal, make sure the server offers you a signature form to sign quickly and quietly.
- Indicate the courses and meals you suggest that adhere to your standards if cost is a concern.
- If the food or service falls short of your standards, apologize to the guests and invitees for the inconvenience caused.

------xxx------

Rules For The Guest

- If you choose not to accept the invitation, do so right away and explain why.
- Otherwise, accept the invitation promptly.
- Understand the venue's guidelines and where the event will take place. Don't be late by more than two to three minutes late.
- When determining what to order, follow what the host recommends.
- Consider how what your order may say about you, and how it may be seen by others.
- Thank the host for the event.
- Say complimentary things about the host that he or she would like to hear but is unable to express about themselves.

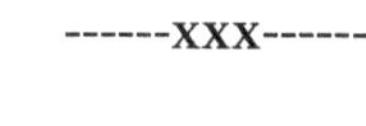

Ordering

- Avoid uncomfortable foods.
- If ordering alcohol is prohibited by business policy, don't do it.
- Be careful when drinking, especially if you want to drive after the meal.
- If you don't want to drink alcohol, never order anything alcoholic.
- Don't get a second drink.

------xxx------

Dining Etiquette

- On each plate, leave some food.
- If a bill is divided, pay it equally.
- No need to bring a doggy bag.

------xxx------

Table Manners

- Do not start eating until your host or guest has taken a seat and begun.
- Put food in your mouth (soup spoon) by bringing it to your mouth, not shoving it inside.
- Take note of other people's eating pace and maintain the same pace.
- Instead of cutting up meat all at once, cut one piece and eat it. Then go onto cut the next piece and eat it, and so on.
- Use the napkin as a napkin; do not use it like a bib.
- Begin from the outside in, and use the silverware in sequence.
- Place silverware in the 10 o'clock position once finished.
- Never dunk food.

- Close your mouth while chewing.
- Talking while chewing food is not recommended.
- If you must speak while there is food in your mouth, avoid chewing.

CHAPTER SIX

Sustained Perception

The four elements of sustained perception are:

- Attitude
- Integrity
- Civility
- Self Discipline

------xxx------

Attitude

Be upbeat about your job, your employer, your peers, your coworkers, your clients, your suppliers, and your company.

------xxx------

Integrity

Never falsify the truth. In fact, following through on your promises demonstrates your level of dependability.

------xxx------

Civility

- Having respect for others
- Sincerity
- Emotional quotient: empathy
- Diplomacy and tact

- Sensitivity to diversity

------xxx------

Self Discipline

- Establishing priorities and planning your time accordingly.
- Prioritizing the significant over the simple.

Providing solutions to client problems

These are some examples of how to treat people as you would like to be treated:

- Sincere Greetings.
- Taking Care of Your Colleagues.
- Combating rumors.
- Managing competitors.
- Graciously accepting criticism.

Diplomacy

Here are some things you may think, but will need to say something quite different, if you wish to maintain diplomacy:

What you think:

- This is going on forever.
- You can't, why?
- I detest it when
- Here's the most effective approach.
- I was too busy, so I didn't complete the study.
- You are so self-centered that you never realise how much you ask for.
- The testing is still ongoing!
- What do you folks do during the day?
- Never pay attention, do you?
- This document is rife with errors.
- Just not going to work.

<u>What you should say:</u>

- How can we fast get this approved (completed)?
- How about you?
- What if it were better if...
- Here is my recommendation.
- I want to finish the study by Friday.
- You're busy, I understand.
- When can we set out 30 minutes to talk about whether to hire a part-time assistant?
- I am aware that these tests demand meticulous preparation and performance. How quickly can you complete it?
- The Director will receive this memo. Please correct the issues I pointed out and thoroughly proofread the report. Thanks. You are a great help.
- Let me express my viewpoint on this matter.

Motivation

Employ words and phrases that can help your listener respond favorably, such as:

- You want what is just for both of us, I know that.
- You'll try your best to assist me, I'm sure.
- My hopes are in you.
- Because you respond to the demands of your department so well, I like working for you.

Responsibility

Ways to take responsibility:

- Putting more emphasis on the opportunities of the future than the issues of the past.
- Employing upbeat language means seeing issues as concerns, issues, or, even better, chances for growth.
- Lastly, and most critically, decide what you can do to modify the circumstance.

Being Pro-Active

Questions that make one wonder what is happening:

- Why does this business not value me?
- Why is it that I can never figure out just how to perform my duties?
- When will I receive the instruction I require?
- Why is there such a lack of enthusiasm among my staff?

------xxx------

Questions that motivate one to make things happen:

- How can I discover the values of management?
- How can I prove my worth?
- How can I learn how to do this work and feel certain that I'm doing it correctly?
- How should I contact my management to bring up this matter?
- How can I communicate to my management what additional training I require?
- How can I acquire the necessary abilities on my own?
- How can I get my staff to share their thoughts on their job with me?
- How can I inspire them more powerfully?

------xxx------

Reframing questions proactively

- Why are things transforming so quickly?
- Why don't things ever change here?
- When will this provider make contact?
- Why is that one customer continually being so rude?
- Why are our services regarded so poorly?
- Why do I work harder than everybody else in my group?
- Why is a coworker of mine so sluggish?
- Why is my boss critiquing my work so harshly?

- Why aren't my employees doing as I tell them to?
- Why must I comply with my boss's requests at all times?
- Why am I unable to adhere to my own job priorities?
- Why am I sick all the time?
- When will this stress start to subside?
- Why is it so difficult to meet people here?

CHAPTER SEVEN

Steps To An Effective Presentation

- Put down all of your thoughts and ideas. When writing, don't stress about the order of your ideas. Simply jot down any ideas that come to you. Consider this topic as much as you can, then write anything that comes to mind.
- Assemble all the information. Make an effort to obtain additional information from a variety of sources, including books, newspapers, and subject-matter experts. Attempt to put all the data on paper or in a word document. Make an effort to organize and arrange all of your information properly.
- Use your personal style. To feel more at ease and free during the presentation as you are utilizing your own style of communication, try to prepare the presentation in your own form of communication.
- Insert Real Examples. Once you are content, try carefully reading the entire presentation a couple of times. In your presentation, try to offer some genuine, worthwhile examples. You can use an example from your own life or one from a book. Yet doing it that way

makes it more obvious to your viewers.

- Fewer alterations. Limit your alterations and only make them when necessary.
- Keep track of how long it takes. Attempt to determine how long the entire lecture will take. Make it brief to stay within the allotted time if it's taking longer than intended.
- Draw attention to the key points. While creating a PowerPoint presentation, strive to bold the most crucial elements and go over the entire thing twice.
- Presentation in PowerPoint. Attempt to deliver your speech using PowerPoint (PowerPoint Presentation).
- Practice a mock presentation. Have a few practice presentations in front of a mirror, friends, or family. Try to keep an eye on your posture and gestures while soliciting input and criticism from your pals.
- Make a recording of your presentation. Review your tone and pronunciation after recording your speech. Try to record your presentation on video if you can.

9 798889 758358

Printed by Libri Plureos GmbH in Hamburg, Germany